SELF
DISCLOSURE

By

JASE L. LINDSEY

For Bettye (Nikie) Lindsey,
Because you told me to chase my dreams
and do what makes me happy.
Making you proud will always be
my greatest accomplishment.
Love, Your Son,
Jase L. Lindsey

Dedicated to Mrs. Eileen Warner
You have always been
and will always be my angel.
You never missed a show and always
provided me an opportunity to shine.
I love you, your "Brownie Brown."

In Loving Memory of Michael
"MJ" Toreano Randolph Jr.
God makes no mistakes,
and although I didn't understand
then, I now know your story was
made to get me here.
I'm doing this for you and all the "MJs"
around the world. Gone, but never
forgotten.
Sleep peacefully, brother.

TABLE OF CONTENTS

INTRODUCTION

THIS BOOK IS TRULY PRECIOUS to me because within these pages, I am able to free myself

And countless others by addressing and speaking the truth on several topics, emotions and struggles that

Young men deal with on a daily basis. I hope that within this book, you will allow yourself to smile,

Laugh, cry, get angry. Ask questions and get answers.

This book is for someone who is lost and looking to climb out of the darkness, but needs a light

To lead the way. This book is for the young man who dares to define the norm,

Pull up his pants and speak to women with the intended respect that they were born with as queens.

This book is for the dreamers who don't give a damn about how society says

You're supposed to live life, but you will live it on your own terms. This book is for the single mothers

Who have raised and are continuing to raise successful men in today's society.

I have always thought of you as the most intelligent women in the world. This book is for you, the reader, whom although I may not know, I consider a dear friend and confidant as I reveal my story, your story, our story of trials, success, emotions and a true desire to be all things pure, classy, timeless, sexy,

Spirit-filled, father figure, and above all, a gentleman. Remember

- Chivalry is SEXY.

"Be joyful in hope,
Patient in Affliction
Faithful in prayer."
Romans 12:12

CHAPTER 1

COMMON GROUND

IT WOULD BE EASY FOR me to begin this book and talk about how I wanted to be a gentleman, the steps I took to attain that goal and how successful it has made me. However, I feel that would cheat you; and in order for us to become acquainted, I feel it necessary to discuss what life threw at me and how I was able to conquer those obstacles. It's also imperative for me to discuss the God-given talents I was blessed with and how these tools helped shaped me into the person I am today.

My childhood initially was the ideal childhood for anyone. Two parents, big house with a huge yard and a dog to match. I had the typical annoying and rough big brother, Jabriel, and a tattletale of a sister, Joni. Sounds pretty normal, right? Life allowed this movie to play for 12 years. I've always been amazed at the pure innocence and carefree spirit of kids, and how they can be completely oblivious to the world and their surroundings. I have always valued the importance of family. I admired my mother and father as a couple and enjoyed watching them laugh, play and shower each other with affection. Everything that we did was in the spirit of togetherness. The house woke up together, had meals together and easily communicated with one another. Weekends were saved for movies and game nights. Our house was the hangout spot for all of our friends. Everyone loved how fun and creative my parents were. Board games, Chinese takeout, sports or a bonfire were just some of the events they would plan for us. Anyone and everyone was welcomed into our house and instantly felt like they were home upon entry. Holidays were very special in our family as well. My favorite was Valentine's Day. When everyone came home and all homework was complete, we would dress in formal attire and would have a candlelit dinner. My father taught my brother and I how to pull out a woman's chair, and our mother showed us how to slow dance and importance of treating a woman right. We also had a prime example as we watched our father shower our mother with adoration and affection. In my eyes, my world was perfect. I knew this was how life was meant to be, and also dreamt of the day when I would grow up and have the same with a family of my own. I became a hopeless romantic at the tender age of 10. After our family prayer at night, I would lie my head on my pillow and drift into sleep with the satisfaction of knowing my world and everything in it was the way it should be. Life, however, would give me a different view at the age of 12.

> *"All divorce does is divert you.*
> *Taking you away from everything*
> *You thought you knew, and everything you*
> *thought you wanted, and steering*
> *You into all kinds of other stuff*
> *like discussions about your*
> *Mother's girdle and whether*
> *she should marry someone else."*
> — MITCH ALBOM:
> "FOR ONE MORE DAY"

> *"Bushwhacked, I examined my hands.*
> *Same hands.*
> *Rings still there, but no longer valid.*
> —SUZANNE FINNAMORE:
> SPLIT: A MEMOIR OF DIVORCE"

Divorce has a smell. A feeling like a dark spell that has been cast over life, and it consumes anything and anyone caught in its gravitational pull. At first, to hear an argument amongst my parents was always a tough thing to endure because they were so rare. At least to my knowledge they were rare. But as I laid my head to sleep at night in my pleasant reality, the make-up and disguises my parents put on for the kids would come off, and the ugly truth would run rampart like a demonic beast in the house under a veil of darkness. A man who I had revered to be a loving, respectable father and an amazing husband was truly a facade. Although I honestly felt he loved and cared for his family and did his part to provide for children, his feelings were not the same regarding his marriage and toward my mother. He spent a great deal of time badgering my mother about how she wasn't as appealing as other women due to her size and appearance, and was pretty open about entertaining other women. Sexual infidelity never came up as an issue, but the love and adoration that was due to my mother was displayed as a feast to other women. My mother had to scrape up the crumbs and be satisfied with what was left. I remember when my father fell sick after cutting his arm on a rusty nail and contracting a bad virus that left him bed ridden and burning with fever, my mother waited on him hand and foot without faltering and continued to shower him with love and affection. His appreciation was displayed by a phone call from another woman to our residence completely insulting my mother. At one point, my mother was an overweight woman, and he reminded her of her shortcomings as he had no desire to be with her intimately and how her lack of appeal hindered him sexually. Although initially, arguments were rare in our house, they soon became the norm and I taught myself to tune them out. I remember waking up in the middle of the night for a glass of water, and found my father sleeping on the floor in the living room. He told me he was having back problems and it helped soothe him. He would continue to have "back problems" for an entire year. Visits by the lawyer became a daily ritual. I truly couldn't grasp the nature of the situation at first, and was unaware that the world I loved was slowly being taken away from me. My brother and father began to be at odds with one another. My brother, who has always been wise beyond his years, felt the tension and understood the situation that was going on. He instantly sided with my mother and lost all respect for our father. I remember them having an argument so intense that my father grabbed Jabriel's arm to control him, but my brother snatched away instantly and jump at my father. His fists were balled and his eyes were bloodshot — anticipating what was next. I grabbed the phone and ran under my bed frantically calling my mother to come home and deal with the situation. Even though we all still resided under one roof, the togetherness of my family was gone, and life in the house seemed force. I began to spend more time at my grandmother's and aunt's houses than I did at home. My parents started attending counseling with the priest at our church. My mother was ready to fight tooth and nail for her marriage, but my father wasn't interested. Especially since one of the women he was involved with happened to attend the same church. He had checked out the marriage a long time prior, and his ring was just a receipt of services rendered.

My escape from this madness occurred between the hours of 9 a.m. and 3:55 p.m., Monday through

Friday. Academically, I wasn't interested in school because my mind was trying to process the confusion and turmoil that was going on at home. School was a chance to hang out with friends, play basketball and regain a shred of my innocence that hung pathetically on the hinges of life. Ultimately, I ended up repeating the 7th grade. The divorce was so heavy mentally and emotionally because it was happening in a space that I knew to be safe; the place where I was loved, nurtured and shown how a husband and wife should come together to love one another and take care of their children. All of those things had been taken away from me. Then there was the battle my siblings and I had to fight with our parents. We were being pulled on both sides as parents were pleading their cases, and we were picked as judges to determine who was innocent and guilty of these transgressions. We were overwhelmed and truly didn't know how to handle these burdens life had given us, let alone pick which parent was the right parent. As time went on, the decision was made for my brother and me. Our father would eventually make the decision to leave the house to relieve some of the tension that was around. He would come by and visit and make sure we were doing what we were supposed to do. Then the visits became very different. He began to only see and spend time with my sister, and for the life of me, I couldn't understand why. I remember one Father's Day, he was coming to pick up my sister for church and to spend time with her. I took it upon myself to get dressed

and be ready and waiting with my sister. I knew he
would be elated and take me along as well. My
mother helped me get ready and watched me wait
for him with excitement gleaming in my eyes. I
stood proud as he pulled up and came to the door. I
stood in disbelief as he left with my sister and left
me standing on the steps — no questions asked. The
final decision came when we attended court one day
(another visit that we had become accustomed to).
After the judge ruled that my mom would have full
custody of the kids, my father told the judge he
would accept responsibility of taking care of my sister and mother, but he would not be responsible for
my brother and me. I couldn't move. I couldn't
breathe. I didn't know what to say or what to think.
A man that I loved, honored and respected told me
he didn't want to care for me anymore. As the truth
set into my heart, my mom felt it was time that all
doors of secrecy be unlocked and that we learn the
very true nature of our family. My mother sat me
down and explained to me that the man I called my
father wasn't my actual father at all. My father was
a man who lived in our hometown of Biloxi,
Mississippi. This man who I had never met surprisingly knew I existed, but had no intentions of knowing me and couldn't have cared less about me. I was
broken beyond measure. Life took my reality, pulled
it from underneath me and left me to figure out the
best way to fall. I couldn't understand how a man
who I knew since I could say my first words, who
celebrated so many of my birthdays, coached

several of my basketball teams, helped me with homework, disciplined me when I was bad and praised me when I did well could just easily walk away from me. Once more, how could a man who laid with my mother, initiated the inception of my birth and was knowledgeable of my existence not care if I was fed, clothed or if my mother could even take care of me. I was falling and from the signs of it, no parachute was attached to me. Luckily I had someone to catch me. In these times of destruction and heartache, I was able to witness and understand the power of a strong black woman. My mother's ship of life was sinking and she began building a raft for us to stay afloat as we watched our reality slip into the abyss. She took the remnant of her heart and dignity and poured it into her children. The mortgage had gone unpaid due to my father and my mother not keeping up with the payments. As we packed up our belongings and went to move into my aunt's house, a feeling of uncertainty swept over me. However, my mother ensured us that everything would be okay. She truly understood the nature of things, not only for herself, but for her children as well. My mother knew that at that moment, her kids were in danger. Society had placed a target on our backs and was ready to throw us into the game of statistics. She knew her two sons were more susceptible to crime and incarceration and had a minimal chance of getting high school diplomas. She understood her daughter was likely to become pregnant by 16 and would barely be able to read beyond a 5th grade level. But my mother didn't give a damn about what society had to say. She was determined to give us everything we needed and present us with every opportunity to ensure we grew up to be successful citizens. Adjusting to this change was no easy feat. It's saddening to know that single-parent households are becoming the norm. There is nothing glamorous about the lifestyle, although I understand I still had it better than some kids. We were blessed to be around an amazing support system. My aunt, who we called "TTKay," cared for us like we were her own children. She bought schools supplies, clothes and Christmas gifts more than anyone. My aunt was also my Godmother so she made sure anything extra I had going on, she would help out. Her son, Terrell, was an additional older brother who I would sneak and borrow clothes from because he had great style. He always watched my siblings and me, and even allowed us to hang out with him. My grandmother, who everyone calls "Big Mama," was more than happy to have us over for the weekends. We enjoyed staying because we got away with murder and she always kept the good snacks. There were countless others from church members to family friends and even teachers who helped my mother with us. I recall one Christmas my mother was struggling to get us things for the holiday. A woman from our church, Dr. Ferguson, was very fond of us, and she told my mom whatever we needed and wanted for Christmas that year, she would pay for it. I am forever grateful to her and many others who showed my mother acts of kindness. Jabriel, who was only a year older than me, helped instill a lot of my values and helped add culture to my life. I don't think he truly knows how much of an influence he was for me. One of the most foundational things my mother did was take us to church. Since their divorce, she had returned back to the Baptist church and we went right along with her. She attended the same church as my aunt, Bethel Missionary Baptist Church in Tallahassee, Florida. My family has always been rooted in faith and I have always loved God. My mother made sure we didn't just go to church, but that we were involved. Our church had an enormous youth ministry, and it was easy for us to make friends. To us, every time we had something to do at church, it was an opportunity to hang out with our friends. But my mother knew she was centering our lives on God. I can't thank her enough for doing so. I truly understand how blessed I was to be in this position given the circumstances of life, but there was true damage that had been done as well. There were constant challenges my mother faced when it came to my brother and me. I know she tried her very best to be father and mother and to fill in from a man's perspective. The saying is true to an extent: "It takes a man to teach a man how to be a man." I give my mother majority of the credit, however, there were pieces that were missing. A deep void was in my life and a deep emptiness that comes when the head of the household is removed from the family. The leader, the one to stand and take charge, to honor and protect, to give direction and provide for his family, and to show his young boys how to become young men. I no longer had this in my life. I was 14, and had no idea who I was or who I belonged to. I had no sense of direction, and the worst part was not being able to understand how I felt or to tell anyone. For a brief moment I even questioned if I was the reason behind my parents' divorce. I felt inadequate and had slipped into a mild depression. I was outwardly happy, but on the inside, I didn't know how I truly felt. Too many questions swirled around in my head and I didn't know where to begin to look for answers. There is a large number of young men who have also had these same problems as me. The most important step is to realize you're hurting and that you indeed need help. My mother took me to a psychologist and at first I didn't understand why. But looking back, I now realized she knew I needed someone to talk to. Even though I would go and not always talk about how I felt, the visits allowed me time to release whatever emotions I felt. Parents, it is so important to talk to your kids after dealing with such a heavy burden. Society has made it nearly impossible for young men to show any type of emotion. By doing so, he is considered weak and helpless. Men are often too worried about being dominant and masculine that we tend to leave our emotions behind. Young men, do not be afraid to express yourself. Even if you don't verbally convey what you are feeling, there is nothing wrong with finding an outlet to release your emotions. I would spend time dancing, playing basketball or fishing. Along with trying to get a grip on my emotions, there was a pattern of behaviors developing that I couldn't explain. I now understand that I learned unwanted behaviors in my life. After Mike, the man I once considered my father, and my mom finalized their divorce, my mom attempted to allow him to have an interaction with us. She felt it was fair because he was the only father we ever knew, and she didn't want to keep us away from him. My brother didn't even entertain the notion and completely shut himself off. I was eager to get my missing piece back. Initially, things started strong. He would come over to help us with our homework or use Sunday dinners as a time to talk and spend time with my sister and me. This consistency lasted for two weeks, and then he stopped coming at all. From time to time, I would call him and ask to spend time or to hangout. "We'll see" is a phrase that I don't use to this day, nor do I like when people say it to me. It was his answer anytime I wanted to spend time with him and more times than not, he wouldn't show up. As these events were happening, unfortunately I was learning what they meant. Through painful repetition and a large serving of disappointment, I learned unwanted skills. Even worse, I began to play them out in my life. I would make empty promises with no intention of following through or start work, but never complete it. It took me until the age of 24 to fully understand the reason behind some of my actions. Subsequently, I have taken it upon myself to slowly break down the walls brick-by-brick and understand the importance of breaking cycles of bad behaviors. I felt free knowing that I was finally aware of my issues and I had the power to control my actions. "You're just like your daddy" isn't a phrase most young men growing up with an absent father like to hear. Most times, we are truly determined not to be like that person and a sense of resentment and bitterness is felt internally. Young men, you have the power to be exactly who you want to be, and just because you have someone's DNA, that doesn't mean you have to be just like them. Take charge over your life, attack your demons head on and get help when you need it. At times, it can be difficult because we have similar traits and behavior patterns from someone we know nothing about. You still have the freedom to be exactly who you want to be, and never look at who they are and think for a second that's how you will be. Make your decision today to master your life and determine your own course. Accepting my parents' divorce was truly a tough pill to swallow, and it took years to accept all that had taken place. With the divorce and turmoil behind us, my mom had found our family a new place to live, and we were all ready to begin a new chapter in our lives.

CHAPTER 2

THE BLUE PRINT

EVERY YOUNG MAN WALKS AROUND with an air of invisibility in the prime of his teenage years. Growth spurts from head to toe, hair sprouting all over our bodies and the attempt to make the little base in our voice deeper than what it really is. The transition from middle school to high school is a rite of passage and one that guys really look forward to. The puppy love relationships of 8th grade are gone, and the girls begin to fill out and develop a womanly shape. High school was the best four years I could ask for as a teenager. From the start, I was determined to put the past behind me, be a new person and make a name for myself. I was set to attend Rickards High School in Tallahassee. My brother was a sophomore there, and his growing popularity helped me to find my way. Before school began, I spent a few weeks of the summer in a high school preparedness program and also trained with the varsity basketball team. I was able to make friends early and get acquainted with the "who's-who" of popular athletes, cheerleaders and many other social groups at the school. At first, I was hesitant to attend Rickards. Up until the 9th grade, the majority of the schools I attended were predominantly white, in regards to the students and faculty, so the transition to an all-black school was intimidating. I was unsure if I would blend in and get along with my fellow classmates. I have always considered myself blessed for being able to make friends easily. I was truly thankful for attending Rickards. The experience helped me to grasp a sense of my identity as a young black man, and also allowed me the privilege to see educators and administrators who looked liked me. These educators often encouraged us to be the best student we could be and to never limit ourselves to what we can achieve. Socially, I learned how to Spades and other card games, and would often quote lines from movies such as *Friday*, *Boyz n the Hood* and others. I also learned how to be quick on my feet when it came to making jokes about someone. For every one joke someone had, I had to have two ready to come back with. And I'll admit, I probably wasn't the best looking brother on campus. I wasn't ugly, but I wasn't one of the muscle-strapped, swag-oozing alpha males either. My "glow up" was still loading. As a result, this made me a bit shy and not too eager to approach girls like many of my classmates would. Because of this, I learned to attract people or gain their interest through my personality and character traits. Dancing was always a way for me to connect to people. Anybody who knew me then and those who know me now could tell you I was always dancing. Performing was always a time when I was confident in what I was doing. Along with dancing, I had a knack for drawing people in through conversation. Even when it came down to approaching a girl at school, rather than giving a couple of corny pickup lines and asking for her number, I would get to know her and see what her interests were. Majority of the time, I was put in that all too common "friend zone." But it was nice to know that I was able to connect on that level. Of all the people I became friends with, I was blessed to gain my best friend around the 6th grade. We met at church, and from then on, we were always together. Hanging out at each other's house, talking about the girls we liked, playing basketball and going to Steak-N-Shake were some of our many traditions we started in high school that have continued to this day. We even went so far as to try and get our moms to move in the same neighborhood when we were in middle school. His name is Darryl, but everyone knows him as "Cookie," a nickname that has stuck with him since it was given to him by my brother and me. Our childhoods were similar, so we became more than just friends — we were great support systems for one another. At times, we could understand what the other was going through without having to say a word. We supported each other at sporting events, and more than anything, we were honest with each other. True, loyal friends are hard to come by, and I was blessed to have found someone like that at an early age. I dealt with the same pressures that any high school student encountered. Wanting to be popular was important, but it was not a big to do for me. I liked the fact that I was known, but I enjoyed the fact that people knew me for me and not because of what I wore or who I was associated with. I dealt with the peer pressure of trying drugs and selling them. I remember sitting in classes watching classmates count wads of cashing while wearing the latest designer clothes and buying whatever they wanted. I was truly tempted to ask and get involved. The pressure was very real, but I understood it was a fast paced lifestyle and I honestly knew it wouldn't be a wise decision in the long run. I watched some of those same guys who sold the drugs and counted the cash become incarcerated and drop out of school. For some, I saw their pictures in the newspaper on the obituary side. A former teammate of mine was selling cocaine and even showed me what it looked like and how much it cost. Afterward, he looked me in my eyes and told me, "You're too smart for this. Stay in school, keep playing ball and get away from here." He passed away almost two years ago. I lost many of my high school classmates due to gang violence, drug abuse, shootings, car accidents and suicide. Of all the funerals, I may have attended one. Not that I didn't want to go, but it was hard to fathom the idea of a casket sitting there with somebody who looks just like me. Or the fact that I had just spoken with someone one day and the next week they were gone. Losing a friend put things in perspective, made me thankful for life and reminded me not to take lightly the opportunities that were given to me. I did exceedingly well for my first year in high school. I stayed on the honor roll and spent countless hours playing basketball. I was determined to be a college hoop star. My hard work earned me the admiration of my peers as well as my coach's. In this, I learned that if I wanted something, I would have to keep working and eventually it would pay off.

Around this time, my mom began introducing my brother and me to older male role models who would take us under their wings. My former next-door neighbor, Mr. Lawrence, and his wife were like older siblings to us and always kept it real with me. Mr. Lawrence helped me get ready for my first major dance and I always confided in him. I never had to worry about being judged and he never sugar coated his answers. They taught me responsibility and accountability by allowing me to babysit their children. My favorite mentors, Marvin and Frantzley Moise, were some of the most influential men in my life. They were my coaches at the local Boys and Girls Club, and took my brother and me under their wings. They taught us to be patient with life and maximize opportunities that were presented. They encouraged us to be gentlemen and would offer advice on style, clothes and the importance of staying well groomed. Our basketball coaches were true father-figures as well. If I missed homework, I was running; didn't clean my room, I was running; and God forbid I made my mother upset. I was really running! Along with the discipline came support and validation. They constantly reminded me to dream and that I could accomplish anything I put my mind to. The mentorship I was receiving was beneficial and I was thankful for each of the mentors God put in my life. My mom once again was the mastermind behind it all. She knew my brother and I were in a very impressionable stage of our lives. We were trying to figure out who we wanted to aspire to be, so she made sure we had positive images and people who taught us to respect her, respect ourselves and to honor God. From elementary until the day I graduated high school, I had very little decision making in my life. Most of my life's choices were already chosen by my mother. She hardly ever entertained what we wanted to do, and she had no desire to be our friend. She made sure to remind us of this as much as possible. We went to church as a family, ate dinner as a family and went out as a family. Privileges were extended on the grounds of chores and homework being completed. It was seldom that I was in serious trouble. I wasn't a bad child, but I was very mischievous. Lying about homework, not doing something when I was told to, hiding dishes under my bed — that was my M.O. Rest assured, my mother had a remedy for that.

Although all her children towered over her, she would gather all the strength her 5-foot 2-inch body could muster and tear us to pieces. My aunts and uncles would often tell her she was being too hard on us. At the time, I agreed. I mean, what kid likes to get beaten? I realize now if she hadn't been so hard, it may have been a correctional officer beating me up. We were allowed to hang out with friends and go to parties, but we had to leave the party before it was over. Who didn't know to be inside before the streetlights came on? My mother was twice as hard because she had little room for error. Raising three kids by herself was truly a daunting task. She made sure she gave each of us more than enough love and affection. I know at times things were truly stressful for her, but she never wavered. She made every basketball game, PTA meeting, recital and anything in between. When I wasn't spending time with my mother or my mentors, I was hanging out with my brother. I would say my brother is the epitome of a good big brother. Older brothers find the younger brother annoying and want very little to do with them. My brother saw me as his equal and for the most part, he always wanted me around. Of course, he had moments when he would shut himself in his room to play with his sacred Army men or listen to classical music, but for the most part, we were side-by-side. One of the greatest things I admired about my brother was his leadership. From birth he was a leader. It was in his nature, and I couldn't see him any other way. He would have the most ridiculous idea like tying our bikes together and riding them, or shooting fireworks at each other, and I would be all in. His persuasiveness was second to none. He talked teachers out of failing him on assignments, and apologized to three girls for missing dates or not calling them all out of the same mouth. The man could wiggle out of anything. He was charming and ugly — well, to me he way, —but girls adored him. He was an athlete and could master any sport in front of him. As popular as he was, he never let it go to his head and remained humble. I picked up confidence and a little cockiness from him. My brother had a great smile, was witty and never felt any girl was out of his league. He could walk up to any girl, hold a conversation, and oftentimes, would leave with her number. He changed women like he changed his underwear. We would have Sunday dinners in high school, and each dinner he brought a new girl to the table. Every time one would say, "I can't wait to come again," I just smiled knowing they had a snowball's chance in hell on returning. I believe only one girl had a three Sunday record until she broke up with my brother, which was a first as well. In the aspect of women, I took the charm and confidence portion, and left him with the rest. My brother also helped instill in me a competitive drive. He was never nice when we played and most of the time, he did his best to humiliate me. I knew if I could beat him, I could beat anyone at anything. We hardly fought, but when we did, we could never stay mad at the other person for more than an hour before we were fooling around again. One thing we definitely had in common was our love for adventure and trying new things. The summer going into my sophomore year, we attended a college preparation program called Upward Bound on the campus of Florida A&M University (FAMU). The program gave us a taste of the college life for six weeks. We lived in the dorms, attended classes and gained the perspective of a student-athlete as the camp organized a basketball team. The program was quintessential because it exposed us to college at an early age. The program was co-ed so everyone mingled well. There were other programs going on and kids from all over Florida came to attend the camps. It was nice to meet people from different backgrounds and schools from around the state. Upward Bound also gave us the opportunity to travel around the U.S. and visit other historically black colleges and universities (HBCU) such as Howard University and Edward Waters College. We visited the Smithsonian in Washington D.C. and took a trip to the White House. The program showed us life outside of Tallahassee, and taught us about art, history and other cultures. I was grateful for this program, and remained a participant until I graduated high school. My sophomore year, I attended Lincoln High School because my brother wanted to run for a solid track-and-field program. As a result, I followed. He adjusted well to the new school, but I struggled. One of my greatest flaws has always been selling myself short. My mom constantly reminded me how intelligent I was and how I could understand anything thrown my way, but I was lazy and wasting my talent. I would go to school and be half interested because I knew if I could understand how the teacher showed me how to do something, I could go home and figure it out for myself. In turn, I would procrastinate on work because I knew eventually I would do it. Ultimately, I would miss work or just not do it at all. To this day, I wish I wouldn't have picked up the habit. I grazed through 10th grade by the skin of my teeth. After that, I decided I didn't want to sell myself short any longer. My laziness caused me to miss an entire season of basketball due to poor grades. Moving forward, my philosophy became "DO WHAT I HAVE TO DO SO I CAN DO WHAT I WANT TO DO!" Junior year, I transferred schools again. This time, my mother got a new job offer and thought it best to keep her eyes on me after last year's performance. I attended FAMU Developmental Research School (DRS). Other than an opportunity to recover from last year, my brother and I were able to play basketball against one another. I was also able to get from under his shadow. He had risen to prominence as a track star at Lincoln High, where he made it to state championships and set records. He was one of the best 400-meter runners in Tallahassee. He even competed in the Junior Olympics in Oregon and was ranked nationally in the 400-meters and 800-meters. I had no desire to walk in his footsteps and the pressure of doing so was released. The funniest thing about attending

FAMU DRS is the amount of time it takes for people to realize there is a new student at the school. By the time I was at lunch, I had been greeted by the entire high school. The school was K-12 and most of the students had been there since middle school. I truly enjoyed how welcoming everyone was and felt comfortable in what could be an uncomfortable situation. I wasted no time figuring out who was on the basketball team and by the end of my first day, I was working out and scrimmaging with the team. I also decided to get involved around campus in various clubs. I choreographed the winter program, Black History Month program and the school's first musical, "The Wiz." My talents and gifts were opening doors for me not only at school, but also in the community. I was being asked to dance for various community organizations. My favorite performance was dancing at graduation for the FAMU DRS class of 2010. I danced with such passion and energy that I received a standing ovation. I was receiving more opportunities and much praise, but I always made sure to stay humble and give God all glory and honor. I have seen so many talented people who were the best at what they did. When they became arrogant and felt self-made, I watched God take their talents from them. That was a constant reminder that no matter how big life made me and how much success I attained, I have to remain humble and thank God for everything. The summer before senior year went by in a blur. I attended a performing arts camp called F.A.M.E. at Fort Valley State

University. A church member who was a fan on my dancing paid for my registration and living fee to attend the camp the previous year, and I won a scholarship to attend the following year. It was an eye-opening experience and truly amazing to be surrounded by other peers who were dedicated to the arts. That summer was bitter-sweet because my brother graduated high school and joined the Army. He was set to leave the week after I checked into camp. The entire day was truly nostalgic. We drove through Georgia, stopping at stores eating lunch, laughing and joking around. It was an emotional day for my mom, but she just watched as we interacted with one another. She knew how close my brother and I were, and this transition in life was going to be difficult for all of us. Looking back, I was thankful I was going to camp that week. I didn't have time to feel sad and think about everything because of the excitement from camp. After settling in my room, my brother and I hugged and he told me to take care of everyone while he was gone. The two weeks of camp went by so fast and my mom was picking me up to go home before I knew it. On the ride home, I looked over the pictures of my brother's swearing-in ceremony for the Army. A wave of sadness was followed by an uncontrollable cry. I knew my brother would be back, but it was hard to fathom living without my partner-in-crime for a while. During his absence, my sister and I formed a stronger bond. Until then, we were notorious for our heated arguments and occasional fights. I lived for annoying her anyway I could. My brother leaving affected her just the same, and we came to an unspoken agreement to support and love one another. We both shared the love of the arts, and that's what truly brought us closer. We shared our dreams and aspirations, and my sister was always telling me to dream big and go for what I want. I also kept my brother's agreement and did my best to help out around the house. I even picked up a summer job to help pay for some of my expenses for senior year. I was selected to be on the Royal Court for my high school and we had quite a few things to buy. We were the liaisons for the school and would attend various functions on FAMU's main campus and throughout the community. We spent the summer learning about etiquette and our roles on the Court. We learned how to eat at a formal dining event, how to assist the girls walking up and down the stairs and the importance of helping them to their seats. Our advisor was a stickler and expected nothing but perfection from us. Most of the things he taught us are tools that I still practice to this day. Senior year, I did everything I could make time for. Along with the Royal Court, I was elected class president and played basketball. I was involved in ministry at church, and everything in life was stable. I fell in love with Fort Valley State University and was very eager to attend the school after graduation. I bought shirts and a tie with the school's colors. I completed the application for the school at least three times before I had one I was happy with. I studied and spent tireless hours making sure I would get a high enough score on the SAT. I was so nervous the day I sent my application off, and I remained anxious as I waited for a response. I checked the mail at least twice a day and eventually my mother banned me from the mailbox. I also applied to FAMU, Hampton University and Florida State University — but had no desire to go. I was a Wildcat at heart and my mind was made up. The day my letter came, I some-how forgot to check the mail. I was at my grand-mother's house and as my mom drove up in her car, she tossed me the mail. I couldn't breathe as I opened the letter, and screamed like a little schoolgirl when I read I was accepted into the university. I took that letter everywhere I went, and showed it to anyone who would look at it. Everything I had worked on the past four years was now validated by my letter. My mom thought horticulture was a good major for me to study, and I gladly went along with it. I would sit and daydream about being on campus and meet-ing new people. The fact that I would be away from home and on my own was definitely an added in-centive. I looked back on everything my family had endured and thanked God for where he had taken us. My mother was happy and she was more than pleased with life. Her children were successful and she loved every day on her job. With graduation upon us, I was eager to begin my new journey of life as an adult.

CHAPTER 3

THE MISSING PIECE

WITH ALL THE SUCCESS AND happiness going on with my life andfamily, God blessed me in a way I could never imagine. During my junior year of high school, my mom began dating a friend of my mentor, Mr. Lawrence. Mr. Lawrence conveniently lived next door to my mother and this particular day he and his friend happened to be outside talking. When my mom introduced us to him, I was skeptical at first. I had watched my mom date a few guys after the divorce and each one fell away and hurt her. I recall her dating one of my basketball trainers for a few years. She truly loved him, and did everything he asked. She always went out of her way to make him happy — cook dinner, help with basketball team fundraiser and attend the games he coached. He played around with my mom's emotions and the ultimate dagger was finding out he was having a baby by another woman. Traveling back to Mississippi after a visit home for Thanksgiving, I watched as my mother burst into tears as she drove down the highway. I was no more than 15 or 16 at the time, and I tried my best to understand her pain. She looked me in my eyes, told me how hurt she was and asked me what to do? I looked on disappointed because I couldn't give her an answer. I didn't know what to say or how to handle the situation. She was left broken and scarred, and I knew I never wanted to see my mother that way again. The new guy had his work cut out for him. Randy Martin was how he introduced himself, and I could see in his eyes he knew this wasn't going to be easy. At 17, I felt like my mom's dad with this "young man" trying to win the heart of my daughter. He surprisingly took the challenge head on, and even had a unique way of going about it. As much interest he had in my mother, he reciprocated the same interest in her kids' lives. The first thing we ever did was play basketball together. A native of Tallahassee, he was a basketball and baseball standout in his time in high school and even spent time in the pros. Being a certain age, I was shocked he still had a little juice left in him to play. I still beat him with ease. He began to show up at my basketball games, and would give me pointers on how to better myself. At times, when my mom had a meeting somewhere, he would pick me up from school. Thanksgiving rolled around and he took me on my first hunting trip. He showed me how to shoot a gun. Although we didn't kill anything, it was a fun and nice to try something new. For Christmas, he helped my mom buy our presents, and spent the entire holiday with our family. Our true connection was my interest in suits and fashion. His profession as a tailor intrigued me. We spent countless hours talking about suits, shirts, shoes and ties. He took me to his shop, measured me for a suit and showed me how to select a quality dress shirt. He would stress the importance of being neat and treating my clothes with care. I always wanted a blue blazer, and he bought my very first one. He also helped me to secure an opportunity to work as a Senate page for Florida Sen. Bill Montford.

Most importantly, he was very God fearing and attended church with our family. He constantly reminded me how I should always keep God first and that with God, anything is possible. I had countless mentors in my life, but he truly separated himself from everyone. Whenever I needed advice, he was the first person I would call. I knew if I ever needed him, he would be there for me. He chastised me when I was wrong, and sung my praise for my accomplishments. The day I met his mother, she showered me with affection and treated me like her grandson. I attended his family reunion, and he introduced me as his son to everyone we met. God had sent me what I wanted for so long and the missing piece of my life was finally filled. It was truly wonderful to have a male role model who genuinely took an interest in my life, and wanted to do anything he could to help me become successful. My senior year, I wore his basketball jersey, number 22, which happened to be my mom's basketball number as well. On my high school's senior night, I decided to show him how much I appreciated everything he had done for me. As they called my name during the game, I wore my last name and his last name on my jersey. I began calling him dad, and he never let me change it moving forward. Even as a young adult, we still find time to share a meal from time to-time, go fishing and talk about our lives and how we want to better ourselves. It was great to finally connect with someone on that level. Someone who recognized that he wasn't perfect and still had work to do. Most importantly, someone who believed in me and never walked out on me when I needed him. I wish more young men could have the opportunity to have a mentor or father-figure in their lives like he is for me. Many young men go astray because they feel as if no one cares about them, and feel like the world is against them. I challenge any gentleman reading this book to find a young man, take the time to get to know him and invest time into his life. It can do wonders to know someone cares about your dreams and aspirations. It encourages you to continue to work hard to be a better person. Most of the time, our youth are watching us, and we have no idea. After Mr. Randy Martin came into my life, I always told myself to give back to other young men in the best capacity I can. True success of a man is being able to go back and give someone an opportunity to better his life like you received.

The best kinds of people are the ones who come into your life, and make you see the sun where you once saw clouds. The people that believe in you so much, you start to believe in yourself. The people that love you, simply for being you. The once in a lifetime kind of people.
Thank you, Randy Martin.

CHAPTER 4

YOUR GIFT WILL
MAKE ROOM FOR YOU

I WAS ONE MONTH AWAY FROM graduation, trying to decide what dorm I was going to move into on campus, when I would start packing for school and looking at courses for the university's horticulture track. Although I wasn't sure about the major, I figured I would like it because my mom suggested it and it is a prominent field. My mom called me into her office, and had one of those "This is serious" looks on her face. I sat down nervously, as she asked me, "Do you know how much it costs to attend this school?" I replied that I did not because I honestly hadn't taken all of that into account. She passed a sheet of paper in front me, and my demeanor changed. I read that the cost of tuition, classes, housing, books, out-of-state fees and meal plan totaled around $28,000 for four years. I had won a few scholarships and knew I was eligible for the Pell Grant and financial aid. However, the look on my mother's face was not so accepting to the cost. She knew I wanted to attend the university, and she wanted me to go as well, but the cost was too high. It was money that we didn't have, and no one had the room to take out a loan. I had been so caught up in my acceptance and how I was going to spend the summer that I forgot reality. I felt like someone had punched me in my stomach. My dream was taken from me in the blink of an eye, and there was nothing I could do about it. My mom tried to make me feel better by telling me to be proud for getting accepted. We had to be financially reasonable, and I would have to enroll into one of the schools in Tallahassee. Graduation came, and although I had a great time with my peers, a part of me was dismissed from life. I spent that summer wandering around and not really caring about much. I dragged my feet about enrolling into FAMU, and my mom forcefully enrolled me at Tallahassee Community College. I was going to class and did my best to become interested in the work, but I had no desire to study horticulture. I found myself displeased with my life, and felt that I wasn't making any choices for myself. It seemed as if I was living how everyone said I should live. The only class that I truly enjoyed and attended regularly was my African Drum and Dance class. Around this time, my mom and I were also bumping heads.

I was trying to figure my life out and somehow gain a sense of independence. She was still being protective and saw me as her little man. I was constantly fighting to get from under her wing. It was difficult for both of us. I had never had a sense of independence and was trying to learn how to go out and do things for myself. I wanted so much to change my major and find something that I wanted to do, but there was I slight fear as to how my mother would react. I would go to my friend house, and she would listen to me complain about not wanting to study horticulture. One day she had enough and asked why I not study the arts?

"You're always talking about your dance class and you put a lot of your effort into," she told me. "It's your passion, so why not pursue it?" Her words hit me hard. I struggled with making a decision for quite some time. I knew sticking with horticulture would mean going through college and graduation, getting a secure job, and making plenty of money. Studying the arts was truly what I wanted to do, but there was an enormous amount of fear. The field is very competitive, and there is never a guarantee that I would always be working. I knew, however, dancing and performing was my passion. I prayed about my decision for the longest time and told my mother that I wanted to follow my dreams and study the arts. At first, she was reluctant, but eventually told me that it was my life and I had to do what was going to make me happy. After our conversation, I felt free and in control of my life once and for all.

Unfortunately, my lack of class attendance caused me to fail my first semester of college. I had the opportunity to make the semester up, but I didn't want to continue my education at TCC. I continued to dance with the African drum and dance group, and picked up a job at the local hospital until I figured what my next move would be. I felt lost. I had the freedom to do what I wanted, but I felt I had no direction. My family wasn't excited about my decision to leave school, and I was constantly badgered about my return. Everything in life was at a standstill and I didn't know what I was waiting for. In the midst of all this, I continued to dance. I danced whenever I got the opportunity and invested my time and energy into my craft. There were so many people questioning my decisions in life, and at times, I didn't understand where all of this was leading. I just knew the only thing that made sense was to keep dancing. I was training in contemporary and ballet and studying different forms of African drum and dance. I began to feel as if I was failing in life and not reaching my full potential. But I wasn't failing at all. I was in a process. Being grounded in my faith, I constantly prayed, went to church and listened to my pastor. He preached about going through the processes of life and how the Lord takes us through things in order to prepare us for his great blessings. He would speak about how we would ask for the blessing, but get weary from the process of attaining the blessing. I took this word and applied it to my heart. Anytime I would get discouraged in life, I would remember that it's all a part of the process. In time, opportunities began presenting themselves out of nowhere. I received an invitation from the Florida African Drum and Dance Festival committee to participate in the festival, attend classes and get taught by some of best dancers in the field. It was an honor to learn and soak up their wisdom. They would speak on staying true to the craft and that if it's your gift, then it will open doors. For the next year, I stayed committed to dancing and getting better. I knew something was coming in due season. I was no longer concerned with the critics outside, and was even beginning to master my own thoughts of disbelief. I decided that nothing was going to get in my way of greatness. Around this time, a former dance mate of mine called me beaming with excitement. She told me she had an opportunity that she wanted me to take. FAMU's Theatre Department was holding auditions for the Color Purple, and she thought I should audition for the musical. At the time, it was November, and auditions were to be held in January. I was currently preparing for the fall show with the African group, and although I thanked her for the opportunity, I didn't give it much thought. A few days later, I found myself opening the package just to see what the requirements for the audition were. Sixteen bars of a song and a minute monologue were needed for the initial audition. Callbacks would be made for those who passed. After that, you would learn 32 counts of choreography. As I looked over the requirements, a reassuring feeling came about.

I'm a firm believer that when God wants us to move, he'll make sure we do just that. I was still preparing for my dance show, but in my spare time, I would practice a song for the audition and learn to read sheet music. I had never done a monologue before, and decided to recite a poem as the equivalent. I found the soundtrack from the play, and annoyed everyone in my house with my constant repetition of the playlist. The day of auditions I was excited and intimidated all at once. I heard about the great talent at FAMU, and for a brief moment, I doubted my skills and ability to compete. The fact that this play was one of the most prominent Black musicals on Broadway was added pressure. I walked into the room and found myself surrounded by other actors and dancers all preparing for their audition. I thought about the students I would be competing against who had been in the program for quite some time and how they might have been more skilled than me. I calmed myself immediately and thought about all the hard work and training I did to get to that moment. I also had my good luck bag of gummy worms, which was a tradition I started while playing basketball. Going over my song and poem, I reminded myself I was there and that I was the best at what I do. It's so important to believe in yourself. We can't expect others to believe if we don't believe first. The audition was nerve wrecking, and as I went through my poem and song, I was truly confident. The judges thanked me for my time and told me callbacks would be posted the next day. I felt accomplished as I walked out the room knowing I had given everything I had in the audition. The next day, my mom called me while I was at work, and I nearly lost my job as I screamed with excitement. I had made the callbacks. I nearly caused my patient to fall out of her bed with my boisterous noise. Callbacks were on a Saturday at 10 a.m. We spent the first half singing and learning the choreography before the auditions would begin. As far as the singing was concerned, I could hold a note, harmonize and maybe give a run or two, but I was not one for solo pieces. I was more than happy when it came to the dance portion of the audition, as the piece we learned was an African-based routine. By the time we finished the auditions, even some of the other dancers came up to me and asked where I had learned to dance. The judges went to their office to make the final cast list. As I waited, I couldn't do anything but thank God for the moment. With much excitement, I looked at the cast list and saw my name listed under the male ensemble list. When I told my mother the news, she fought back her tears and told me how proud she was of me. She told me she admired my dedication to my craft and how I could do anything when I put my mind to it. As we prepared for the show, I gave all of my energy and focus to the show. I was in a new environment, and eager to soak up the knowledge. In my eyes, the FAMU Essential Theatre is the epitome of a college fine arts department. The professionalism and discipline I learned during the rehearsals were things I had never experienced. All actors were required to be on time for rehearsals. Most of the time, on time meant to be early so that we could have a pre-warm-up before the actual warm-up and rehearsal. The rehearsals were fun, but intense and highly competitive. Roles were being filled and no one was shy about saying they could do a part better than another person. Our choreographer had selected me to begin the dancing in the opening number of the play. I knew I had one shot to get everything right, and all eyes were on me as I was one of the few actors cast who was not in the program. I executed the choreography flawlessly and gained the admiration of my colleagues. As rehearsals progressed, I began to get to know everyone and started spending time with the cast outside of rehearsals. I knew it was important to develop friendships so that the overall chemistry of the play would flow. We went to parties, played spades, told jokes and really enjoyed getting to know one another. Brandon Heyward was my partner-in-crime, and he really made me feel comfortable. He gave me advice on the show, encouraged me to work on certain things and even asked me to consider enrolling into the program. I would come to rehearsals early to help out with the sets and to learn more about the theatre. I also began to develop a relationship with the faculty, especially the director of the show, Mr. Luther Wells. He appreciated my energy and dedication, and we got to know each other very well throughout the production. As the show date came closer and closer, we became the talk of Tallahassee.

The tickets were selling rapidly, and everyone was excited about the show. Opening night was a red carpet event and everyone was dressed in formal attire. My entire high school came during one of the runs of the show, and former teachers told me how proud they were. Teachers, church members, friends, family, everyone I knew supported the show. And, they all would wait until after the performance to congratulate me and tell me how proud they were. Each night the show improved and everyone gave 100 percent. One show I injured myself during a transition of props, and had to sit out the rest of the performance. I refused to miss the next show and pushed through to give one of my best performances. After the show was over, and everyone was saying goodbye, Mr. Wells spoke with my mother and me. He told me how he watched how dedicated I was to the show, and how he never had anyone from outside the program put in so much effort. He told me I was gifted, and he wanted to help grow and mature my gift. He offered me a spot in the program as well as scholarship money to help with expenses for school. My mother and I stood there stunned. We gladly accepted his offer and called everyone to tell them the news. I went home, cried and thanked God for the rest of the day. Everything I had gone through finally made sense. The decision to pursue the arts, the countless hours and dedication into my craft, the resilience to stay on course and not give up — it was all worth it. I was thankful for my friend who presented me with the opportunity to audition, and God's guidance to stay committed. Life had truly come full circle for me, and I was truly amazed at how my gift made room for me. I was going to be in a space where I was passionate about what I was doing, and I knew it was the right thing to do. God's timing is always perfect timing. Never give up on something you believe you were born to do. Even when life doesn't make sense at times, continue to believe in yourself, and to stay hungry and focused. Learn to tune out the disbelievers and critics, and be your biggest fan! If something is for you, God will make sure it's given to you and make sure that you are prepared when he does bless you. Whatever you do, don't QUIT.

CHAPTER 5

20:1 RATIO

COLLEGE, THE BEST FOUR YEARS of life — or at least that's what we are told. An opportunity to be independent and out on our own; scheduling classes to our liking, staying out late and cramming until the wee hours of the morning. You're chilling in the dorm one minute and the next, you're at a party. In my case, there is no better college experience than that of an HBCU. Here you get the college experience, but there's an added incentive. You're surrounded by "Black Excellence" everywhere; from peers to professors and the constant reminders of how proud you should be to experience this great institution. There is no better HBCU in this nation than the one that sits on the highest of seven hills in Tallahassee. My mother graduated from FAMU and pledged, in her words to the "real" Beta Alpha chapter of Delta Sigma Theta Sorority, Incorporated. My aunt was a professor at the school, and I spent countless years attending homecoming and other campus events. However, the true college experience is second to none when it's time to attending the school. I assumed because I was 21-years old, I wouldn't be so eager, naïve and immature as an 18-year old freshman. I was correct in the sense of immaturity, but wrong with the other two. The first week of school was amazing. It was filled with social events, different organizations and countless new faces. I met someone new everyday on campus. Early on, I decided I should join a campus organization. Since dancing was my thing, I chose to join the world renowned FAMU Strikers Dance Troupe. You may remember seeing them perform on America's Best Dance Crew Season 3. I also would meet my life-long friends and roommates, Stefan Bayne and Sharard Saddlers, while in this organization. During my tenure, I would get into a world of foolishness with these two —parties, late night study sessions, heated arguments and women. Stefan never lost an argument because he somehow always found a way to make his point valid. Now by this time, you may be wondering why I named this chapter after a mathematical term. The 20:1 ratio has less to do with math and more to do with women. On the campus of Florida A&M University, the ratio of men to women is 20 to 1. For every one male, there are 20 females. As you can imagine, for any decent looking man, those numbers sound amazing. I'm here to tell you that hearing it does not compare to seeing it. The first thing I remember saying when I walked onto campus was, "There are a lot of fine women here!" I was completely surrounded. They were everywhere — classes, library, coffee shop, gym, parties, you name and there were beautiful women. Most of the guys on campus tend to group together, and are identified by who they hang with. The term "juice" was applied to a group of guys who had the swag and individual personalities that were cool. "Lames" were…..well….I'm sure you can figure it out. Our group had juice, and with the juice comes the women. Most guys on campus on average talk to three to five ladies at one time. Nothing ever too serious, strictly entertainment. They do this to figure out which one was worth settling down with. Most of the time a guy would get so wrapped up in the entertainment that settling down was never a thought. Not to mention, if you ever fell out with a girl, you could always meet someone new, after all, 20:1. At first, I wasn't so eager to talk to the girls because I spent the first two weeks of school just going to class and going home. By the time I made friends and joined the dance organization, that's all the conversations were ever about. If women could be flies on the wall of a male dorm room or apartment for a day, I think they would lose their minds listening to the conversations. We talked about anything — what girl had the biggest butt, who was fine and who wasn't, what girl was the freak of the group and the list goes on. Guys saw the campus as a playground, and were eager to see which swing could go the highest. Initially I wasn't caught up in the hype, but the more we went to parties and hung out on campus, the more I could see what they were talking about. There's something that makes a man walk taller when he's on campus and a woman calls his name, gives him a hug, or stops talking to someone else just to speak to you. The fact that you could meet a new girl every day of the week was also mind blowing. One day you meet Tyesha who's studying theatre, the next you are meeting Brittany in the College of Pharmacy. After a while, guys broke it down to a science. If you talked to five women, you made sure each girl was from a different city, studied a different major, and never knew each other or ran with the same group of friends. A check of an Instagram or Facebook account told a guy the basis he needed to know about a girl and who she hung with. The more girls a guy talked to, the higher chance of getting caught. And some of the drama I witnessed on campus was second to none — cars getting keyed, clothes thrown out of windows, fights and surprise pop ups. Most guys lived for the drama, and we all loved telling stories about how crazy a girl was. Keeping count of sexual encounters was also a big to do in a group. I won't go into numbers on the average, but I will admit to hearing some pretty outrageous numbers, and how guys would argue if someone was being honest or not. I can truthfully say I know I guy who considers one of his crowning achievements is having relations with a girl from every club and organization on the campus. What guys really lived for were freshmen. A fresh new group of girls, young and naïve. Most of the play went to guys in the fraternities, followed by the dance organizations and then athletes. The Pajama Juice Jam by the Sigmas, and Mardi Gras hosted by the Omega's brought the ladies by the hundreds. And all the guys went to scope the talent and sip on the juice. My group was no exception to any of this. We had fans, and many of the guys had girls who would fall out just by seeing them. I was the ugly one in my group… OK, I am lying, but I wasn't foaming at the mouth at the ladies as some of the guys were. In terms of relationships, most guys had the main, bae and side ideology. If you're unfamiliar with this philosophy, I will break it down in the chart below.

MAIN	BAE	SIDE PIECE
Girlfriend	Not a girlfriend, but has potential	Not even close
All rights reserved to hold title and to post pictures on all social media's, and mark in a relationship on Facebook.	If a main is not in play, can post occasion MCM (Man Crush Monday) on social media, and show on Snapchat every now and then. No Facebook.	No rights reserved, doesn't care what you do. No social media posting, can only like select amount of pictures.
Potential wife	Has to make it out of Bae phase to become girlfriend before going further.	More than likely, promiscuous, so no consideration for any type of status.
Met the parents; went on vacations	May know mom and talk to her on the phone once a week.	Phone number is saved under a different name; doesn't know anyone?
All major purchases, all holidays, shoes, clothes; allowed at the apartment or dorm room anytime	Christmas and Valentine's day gifts if discussed; if calls in advance, allowed to come over. Maybe dinner on occasion and a date.	No gifts ever unless buying for him, but don't expect anything back. Only comes over when is called upon, usually after 10 p.m. No public appearances with each other.

As shocking as that may be to some, that's the exact science of how women are placed into categories in college. I'm sure some ladies who are reading this book are shocked to find out which category they reside. It's truly unsettling knowing that is the view on women, but I hope it provides insight. I am not exempt from the use of that chart, and I will admit that I have used all three categories at different points of my life. Initially, I wasn't so wrapped up in the girl because I was 21, in school to get my education and that was it. When I started hanging with my friends, I eventually started talking to a few, but I never considered anything really going too deep with any of the girls. The girl I actually fell for, I met in a class I wasn't supposed to be in. Freshmen take a College Success course, and mine was scheduled for 2:30-3 p.m. on Mondays, Wednesdays and Fridays. On the first day of class, there was no professor and only I and another student came. An advisor showed up and told us the class had been canceled, and we had been moved to different class. At first, I was just in the class, did what I had to do and then went home. But as I got involved with the Strikers, I had to publicize and tell people about the events. One particular day, I was tapped on my shoulder by a brown-eyed, long-haired, soft-spoken angel. She had overheard me speaking to someone and asked me if I was trying out. I politely said yes and she told me she was trying out for the sister organization, Mahogany Dance Troupe. I thought that was pretty cool, From then on, I began to sit by her and her friend in class.

Eventually, I asked for her number, initially not really thinking anything of it. Then we started texting and hanging out. I slowly found myself interested in her. She was a dancer, well traveled and very classy. The fair came around, and I asked her a thousand times to go with me, but she never gave me a straight answer. I found out from her friend she had a boyfriend at the time. When I asked why she didn't tell me, my heart skipped a beat when she told me it was because she liked me. In time, her relationship would end, and we continued getting to know each other. The Sunday before finals, I asked her out while sitting in a booth at McDonalds. I remember the first thing I ever bought her was a medium pineapple mango smoothie and a medium fry. We studied together all exam week, and even got up early to eat breakfast the last day of exams. The day she was leaving to go home, I ran across the school in a full suit to say goodbye, and to meet her dad. I was thankful I was in a suit when I met him, because I figured it would help with the impression. I prepared to spend my winter break in Texas. I was excited because I had someone to call my own and think about during the break. As I stared out the window in the car, I couldn't be happier. Until my phone vibrated...

GF: Hey Stranger!!
Me:..................Sup
GF: You just forgot about me since school huh?
Me:.............................
I guess I did forget.

CHAPTER 6

PERFECT IMPERFECTION

I heard you're a player, so let's play a game.
Let's play-fight. Let's sweet talk
Let's talk and text 24/7.
Let's tell each other good morning and goodnight
every day.
Let's take romantic walks together. Let's give
each other cute nicknames.
Let's hangout with each other's friends.
Let's go on romantic dates.
Let's hug and kiss.
And who ever falls in love first?

Loses.

DISCLAIMER:

Beyond this point lies a true story. A story of a flawed individual and his perfect imperfections.

At one point in time, this person would consider himself one of the worst in the world. He chose a period of time to break hearts and to play with emotions without losing a wink of sleep. Damaging others without so much as batting an eye and not an ounce of remorse for his actions. In no way do I, nor the character spoken about in this chapter, condone any of these actions; nor are we proud of what has taken place. To keep the privacy of all persons involved in this chapter, names have been changed. From this point until the end of the chapter, there is nothing good to say. However, "Even a good player will someday become a toy of a better player. It's called Karma."

She had no interest in him. She loved him, but certainly not the same anymore. She was exhausted, mentally, physically, emotionally exhausted. "Four years," she said it quietly with an air under her breath. Janae looked at herself in the mirror. She didn't even recognize who she saw. Of course the reflection was hers, but inside she couldn't see herself. "Four years." This time she said it louder in a tone of disgust. She didn't deserve this and he didn't deserve her. He spent his time once again doing the same old thing and having the same old excuses. She knew his routine from every head scratch to eyebrow raise and the obligatory "Wow!" when he couldn't believe what he was hearing. "Why am I still here?" Janae was pacing. Now the questions popped in her head in a fury, leaving him no time to answer them. Flashback of his late night entrances, silently showering and hoping in her bed as if nothing was wrong. She was never really asleep, but she was tired of being slept on. She couldn't understand his actions at all. Honesty and loyalty had been given since day one. She gave her all to him and never wavered in her faithfulness. Sure he had his moments when he was sweet, and for a time, he would be the perfect gentleman and there would be no problems. Never lasted no more than two months or so before a new problem arose. When the odds were stacked against him and the world was cold, she was there to protect him. When he had nothing, she never complained. When he was in between jobs for a month, she never wavered and even encouraged and helped him to find a job. He showed his gratitude with the same old routine. Janae just couldn't understand. "What do they have that I don't?" The answer was, "Nothing." She had everything right and he couldn't see that. She was the one every man posted about on his Instagram, and some would get on their knees and pray to God to send their way. He was blind. "He met my family" was another thought in her mind as she put on her bikini and headed out the door. He did more than just meet her family. He knew her family. He spent countless hours speaking on the phone with them. Last summer, they even traveled and enjoyed a vacation together. This summer was no different as a trip to the family reunion happened a month ago. He spent time with her father and mother quite often. He was able to joke and speak as freely as he wanted with them. It should have made sense to him, but it didn't. Janae was willing and considering marriage. Willing to play the fool to say she's in love. The fool? Now she had to reconsider. She had played the fool long enough. Even at the moment as she stood on the white sandy beach of the Dominican Republic. A beach that he should have been standing on right next to her, after all the trip was his idea. It was his birthday and she was standing alone on the island. She felt alone. She boarded the plane alone and arrived at the hotel in the middle of the night all alone. Happy birthday wasn't necessary. This trip was important to her because he was losing and he didn't even know it. Last week, she hoped this trip would have been the spark they needed. She had left her phone in the hotel room. She needed to. The constant buzzing and long obligatory "I'm sorry" from a sad and undeserving boyfriend were coming in like breaking news. He was promising how things were going to change and professing his love as fast as his fingers could type.

It didn't matter anymore. He didn't matter anymore to her. It was her time to think. For so long, she had put him first and the relationship first that she had lost herself. It was time to consider herself, after all, a queen has to take a step back and adjust her crown every now and then. Janae stared at the crystal clear water, and for the first time in a long time, she saw herself. A slight grin came across her face, and as the wind blew a soft breeze over her body, she knew what she had to do. Sick and tired of being sick and tired was an understatement. It didn't matter anymore. She knew who she was now and knew what she brought to the table. "He likes to play games, so I'll play mine," she thought to herself. "I know I can play better." This wasn't a game out to hurt or be cruel, but a game to put an end to a game. His world was about to come crashing down and he had no idea. Too many dudes had been curved, too many disrespectful comments had been put into check and too many fake phone numbers had been given out. It was time to take back what was hers. She knew he loved her, but he didn't love her correctly and she couldn't let him continue to damage her any longer. She considered herself "Da Baddest," and she was going to act like it. She was thankful for the getaway. For the first time in a long time, she held her head up high and felt all the confidence in the world. She fixed her crown and promised herself to never lose it again.

Freedom.

Freedom - The power or right to act, speak or think as one wants without hindrance or restraint.

You don't love me deep enough
We not reaching peaks enough
Blindly in love, I fucks with you
Until I realize I'm just too much for you,
I'm just too much for you.
                              - BEYONCÉ:
                    "DON'T HURT YOURSELF"

You didn't love her. You just
didn't want to be alone
Or maybe, maybe she was just
too good for your ego.
Or maybe she made you feel better about
your miserable life, but you didn't love her
Because you don't destroy people you love.
                    -GREY'S ANATOMY-

Everything about this amazing woman was right, and I was completely wrong. I was wrong to ask her for her phone number, and spend hours of time talking to her on FaceTime, telling her corny jokes, and asking her what her favorite foods and colors were. I had no business asking about her likes and dislikes, about where she has been in the world, and where she wanted to go. I was entirely unsuitable to want to know about her hopes, dreams and aspirations in life. Who was I to have the audacity to ask if she had been hurt before, and the gall to allow her to open up and divulge her inner most secrets to me? I should have never opened the door in the manner I did. I should have checked myself, but the problem was, I was blind to my own mess. I was blind before her, I was blind as a child, and I was too young to realize it.

As I stated earlier in the book, I deemed myself a hopeless romantic because of the love and relationship my mother and stepfather had put on display for me. I admired their relationship, but lack of commitment and years of waiting caused my mother to be fed up. I have seen a lot of beautiful things break in my life. It was a rare occasion for me to be around a happily married couple or to see a "normal" family. Most of the time, when I was around it, it was overwhelming because I wasn't accustomed to the environment. It was no longer familiar territory and for a time, I felt it wasn't for me. I had no idea how to love someone. My mother had preached to my brother and me about respecting women, and to treat them how we would want someone to treat her. I had never seen my mother be treated with a modicum of the respect, love and adoration that she deserved. Everything that I saw growing up either faded away or was a lie. The role models I had truly taught me how to be a gentleman, but we never had conversations about love and monogamy. I guess they were trying to figure it out for themselves, and thought it wise not to give me any pointers. I did the best I could to piece an idea of what love should be. My first serious relationship lasted five years, but only two of the five were actually full of love and happiness. The other three years were spent in a love triangle with her, her ex-boyfriend and her nosy friends. Sub-tweets, random phone calls and rumors were an everyday thing for a solid three months. After the drama came her indecisiveness as to whether or not she still loved me and wanted to be with me. I flew clear across the United States with her to show I still cared. I gave her an ultimatum, and her first response was no. I should have left her with that answer. The last year we spent together, we weren't together at all. History and familiarity was all that was left, and we rarely spent time with each other anymore. The love had faded, but neither one of us knew how to part ways. To make matters worse, we had both become interested in other people. I knew for quite some time that she was attracted to a friend of mine, and I knew that they had already been spending time together. As a result, I felt justified in my actions when I did meet someone new. My ex tried one more time to put life in our relationship, but I had given up completely by that point. I was infatuated with Janae, but she couldn't pay to get my attention. I wouldn't say that the grass was greener on the other side, but I just had no intention on cultivating my own landscape. I felt it was no longer my job to care and she would figure it out eventually. If she didn't, I couldn't have cared less. I know I was completely wrong for my thought process. Rather than manning up and ending the relationship, I just let it sit and rot from the inside out. In all honesty, I have never broken up with anyone in my life before. Suffering from detachment problems, I was never comfortable with dismissing someone from my life. To me, the pain was equivalent to the way I felt when my stepfather left me, and I didn't want to do that to anyone else. Of all my actions, the worst was bringing a beautiful woman into all of my mess. A woman, who truly adored me with the upmost regard, saw me completely hers and valued the innocence of our relationship. I tainted it from the very beginning. Every ounce of me wanted to commit to her and I was falling for her, but I was unable to give her all of me because I was hiding an ugly secret that I didn't know how to let go. Eventually, my ex and I did sit down and agreed to part ways. Finally freed of the situation, I knew I would be able to care for Janae. Unfortunantly, I forgot about the baggage that I was carrying. I should have taken time to fully let go of everything and spend time alone, but I was trying to fall in love again. My lack of handling business would cause me to have a moment of infidelity, as I was weak and easily tempted. I ran and gave the necessary "I'm sorry, she doesn't mean anything to me," and "You know I only love you" routine, as any man would do when he's caught. She stayed with me, and I knew she was really in love with me. If I could go back in time and speak to her, I would tell her to leave my sorry behind right there. She took the innocent sheet of our relationship that I had tarnished and did her best to blot out the stain. The blemish faded, but the sheet wasn't the same, and she accepted it. I had no business being with this wonderful woman. I was doing anything I wanted to do, and she forgave me time and time again. Girls would text my phone and my response was, "I can't control these girls. They are grown." I had every right; in fact, it was my duty to text these girls and tell them I had a girlfriend. I liked the attention, and I entertained them from time to time, even though I knew I didn't want to be with them. I remember she was upset after I didn't call her to say I wasn't sleeping at her place after a party. It wasn't that my phone was dead or anything. I was drunk and didn't care. I figured she could put two and two together. I didn't see it as a concern for my wellbeing and her concern as a girlfriend to make sure I was safe. I saw it as being annoying. Janae put so much time and effort into our relationship, and she supported every one of my dreams and aspirations. I remember speaking about taking a cruise for my birthday. The next day, she had a travel agent, itinerary and made the first down payment for our cruise. Joined by her parents and sibling, we enjoyed a four-day vacation in Mexico. I was completely blown away. I had never met anyone who invested in me as she did. Even times when I wasn't sure how my life was going to play out, she stood by me and encouraged me to find a way to make my situation better. I displayed my gratitude by doing the same things over and over, and never owning up to it. When we first met, I didn't have a dime to my name. She paid for everything and never complained once. I took her for granted. I truly messed up when I allowed her to go on our planned vacation for my birthday alone. Rather than being responsible and getting my passport on time, I tried to scramble to get it done at the last minute. Her parents were furious with me and they had every right to be. We had planned this trip well in advance and I had enough time to get the necessary things done. Once more, I was trying to show her I truly loved and cared for her when she came back from the trip. But by this time, she wasn't paying me any attention. I was trying to force my love and affection on her, and it wasn't accepted. The true breaking point came when we both decided to go out one night and we ended up at the same club. That day, I had agreed to give our relationship a break. While at the club, I got belligerently drunk, and was trying to be around her. I grabbed her phone and was highly upset to find out she had been texting her ex-boyfriend. I completely lost my mind, and began yelling and screaming at her outside of the club. As she turned to walk away from me, I forcefully grabbed her back. In that moment, I knew it was all over. I had never put my hands on her in that manner. The first thing I did was call her dad and told him exactly what I did. A move that I'm sure most guys wouldn't have done, and a move that was truly risky on my behalf. It scared me more than anything because I feared she thought I would have hit her. I eventually sat down with her parents and we discussed the issue. If there was ever going to be a second chance, I needed to confront my mistake head on and apologize to her parents. That had to be one of the lowest points in my life because I have a zero tolerance for abuse on women. For me to act in that manner was ultimately disappointing. It was hard to live with that mistake, and I constantly questioned whether or not I could come back and be a better person. It's true what they say: you never miss what you have until it is gone.

This chapter by far has been the hardest to write because I'm not proud of my actions. Many people tell me "You're young; it's college. It happens." It shouldn't happen. Emotions and feelings are nothing to play with. Being so caught up in my life and doing things my way caused me to lose someone who was truly a blessing. What hurts me the most was thinking about everything that my mom went through, and how multiple men hurt her. In essence, I was no better than they were, and even did some of the exact same things that I saw. I had to sit and question myself and my motives. I realized it was a cycle. A cycle I knew I wanted to end at that moment. A cycle I knew needed breaking, not only for myself, but also for others around me. At the end of the day, I consider myself a gentleman, and I decided that I wanted to carry myself the same way. But it was far beyond wanting it just for myself. It was my duty to save myself and save others. I was willing to take on the challenge. Men, if you have a woman who's willing to go to battle with you, and give you her last, keep her. It's rare to find someone who's selfless and considerate of others. Keep what's real and realize that for every action, there is a reaction.

Right now, I can apologize and offer my
regret. Until you are to see me again
We cannot even begin to move
on from this mistake.
Just give me a chance to show you
that I can be better than this.

-UNKNOWN

CHAPTER 7

THE PERFECT GIFT

If there is one saying I hold very true in my life, it is, "Everything happens for a reason." I am a firm believer in that, and although at times we may not understand it, eventually life shows us why we must experience certain things in life. The good, bad and ugly all make sense at some point. And most of the time, we are appreciative of how things come together. From childhood to this very moment, I know everything in my life has happened for a reason. I didn't know I would write this book and start a business on etiquette, but everything in my life has shown me how I got to this point. Being hurt as a child, finding strong mentors, being "a dog" and meeting amazing people all make sense to me. I truly hope that you have found this book inspirational and entertaining. I wrote this book for guys, because men, we must step up. I truly became adamant about wanting to be a gentleman and educating others when my best friend lost his brother the summer of 2016. It was no more than three weeks after Janae broke up with me, and I was trying to make sense of my life and what I was doing. I was sitting at an IHOP with my friends, Lachelle and Deandre, who were trying to cheer me up. Someone posted on social media about a shooting in a neighborhood, and we really didn't think twice about it because it was common in that area. Then DeAndre was notified that it was my best friend's brother, MJ. I lost my mind. Stefan had gone home for the rest of the summer, and Sharard and I were working together at a pizza joint for the summer. MJ was a quiet, mild mannered guy who got along with everyone, and kept to himself for the most part. The first time I met him, he walked in Sharard's old apartment joking how dirty it was. My favorite memory was the 4th of July when we tried to lighting the grill using $3 charcoal from Walgreens. The last conversation I had with MJ, he told me how he wanted to do better in school, and that he was saving money to get his own place. I called Stefan, told him what I learned. The next call was the best call I ever made in my life. I called Janae. She didn't ask questions. She just asked where she needed to meet me. It was hard being strong for my friend, and I couldn't fathom how it felt to lose a brother. I took Sharard to my mother's house and she helped me care for him. I spoke with his family to let them know what was going on.

It's funny how God will prepare us for something without us knowing what he is preparing us for. After Janae and I broke up, I spent most of my alone time in my Bible and praying for God to show me direction. God was preparing me to be strong and lead my friend in his time of need. Along with God strengthening me, I also found my strength in Janae. When we got to my mom's house, the first thing she did was grab my friend and begin to pray. Up until that point, I cried a little, but I kept it together for Sharard. But then, I fell on the floor in an uncontrollable cry. Janae silently came over, grabbed me by my shirt and told me I had to stop crying and be strong for my friend. I immediately dried my eyes and didn't cry again until I went back home later that night. As the funeral came, and we said our goodbyes, my spirit was troubled. I knew I had to do something to honor my friend's death and to make a change in the lives of young men. I thought about if I would have influenced MJ or showed him more things, maybe he would still be here. His message to me was to save those who are still here. And that's what I intend to do. The AdjuvantGentXperience allows me the opportunity to show young kids and young men that having manners and practicing chivalry can help you be successful in all aspects of life. I had great help from my mentors. I believe the man I learned the most from, and still learn from to this day is Enitan Bereola, the auther of *Bereolaesque*. His book talks about how being a gentleman made him successful. I knew being a gentleman was important, but his book showed me it was cool. I deemed it as sexy, and saw it as a lifestyle and not just a trend. Enitan has gone on to write books for women and relationships, but his first book given to me by Mr. Lawrence when I graduated high school, was the birth of what you're reading today. Men, it's important to be gentlemen, especially toward women. Too many women are underappreciated, and we spend too much time demoralizing and belittling their value. I've had my share of the action, and I quickly learned it was nothing I wanted to continue. I find it more appealing to remind a woman she's a queen and to treat her as such. It starts with how we view ourselves though. We are kings. We are made in God's image. We should sit on our thrones and hold ourselves in that manner. There is a gentleman in every man, and you don't have to change who you are to become one. It all starts in the mind. To the young man struggling to find answers about life, I hope this book can give you some answers. I'm here to tell you, you're going to be OK. To the young man who has made mistakes and wonders if he can bounce back, you can. Change isn't easy and habits are hard to break. Many will ridicule and people love to bring up the past. Let that fuel and inspire you to keep moving forward. Let it serve as reminder that you are better than who you used to be. This book itself is a product of negative living that has been turned around into something truly masterful. Single mom, your sons will be fine. Surround them around greatness and they'll pick up the blueprint. Men, find a young man and make an impact in his life. After all, the goal is to be pure, classy, timeless, sexy, God-like, a father-figure, and above all, a gentleman.

Remember:

-Chivalry is Sexy
- JASE LEON EMMANUEL LINDSEY

ACKNOWLEDGEMENTS

FIRST AND FOREMOST, TO THE Most High God, I thank you for this art. God blessed me with amazing gifts and talents, and to say that I have used every one of them is a blessing. If someone would have told me one day I would write a book, I would have looked at that person crazy. I give all glory and honor to God, and I pray this book inspires many. To my mother, I thank you for being the most amazing black woman this side of the Mississippi River. To my grandmother, Mildred Davis, thank you for your life, and allowing me to pester you with my devilish jokes. Joni and Jabriel, I love you both with all my heart, and y'all are the best siblings a brother can ask for. My Godmother, Carolyn Cummings, thank you for always supporting me and wrapping me in your love unconditionally. All my cousins, aunts and uncles — thanks for your support and prayers. Michael Lindsey, thank you for the life lessons you taught me. I am thankful we have a relationship again. To my biological father, if you ever read this, thank you for giving me inspiration and showing me what kind of father I want to be. My best friend,

Darryl Ward, and his mom, Angela Ward, and sister, Ariel, thank you guys for your support, prayers and countless sleepovers and meals. Darryl, I love you and thank you for your friendship. You are forever my best friend. To Bethel Missionary Baptist Church, the Rev. Dr. R.B. Holmes and the entire congregation, thank you for fueling me with positivity and with God. And thank you for always allowing me to use my gift. To Sharad Tyrell Saddlers, Stefan Bayne, Paul Gordon, the "Hated Eight" of Fall 2K13 Strikers, thanks for being good friends, supporting me and getting into foolishness. To Florida A&M University, Mr. Wells, Dr. Valencia Mathews, Ms. Kimberly Harding and all the Essential Theatre staff and students, thank you for the love and reminders to stop selling myself short. To Ms. Carol Curry, thank you for always giving me opportunities to grow and share my gift. To the entire city of Tallahassee, Florida, affectionately known as "The 850" and many other names, thank you for allowing me to grow up in this city and not grow up too fast. I learned a lot living in Tallahassee and I wouldn't trade this place for anywhere in the world. To Mr. and Mrs. Roker, thank you for being amazing and showering me with love and providing an example of a strong God grounded and loving marriage. I aspire to have a marriage and relationship that reflects yours. Finally to you, the reader, Sir, Ma'am, Bro., Sis., or however you choose for me to address you. Thank you. Thank you for taking a chance, picking this book up and reading the pages. I hope my story has affected you in a positive manner and gives you hope for brighter days. There's a saying I found, on the Internet that I truly love. "You've already survived some of your worst days ever, so keep going." Please keep going. And remember, anything is possible with GOD.

Made in the USA
Columbia, SC
16 April 2019